LEARN GERMAN FOR KIDS

LEARNING GERMAN FOR CHILDREN & BEGINNERS HAS NEVER BEEN EASIER! HAVE FUN WHILST LEARNING! FANTASTIC EXERCISES FOR ACCURATE PRONUNCIATIONS, COMMONLY USED PHRASES & VOCABULARY!

PRO LANGUAGE LEARNING

© Copyright 2020 - All rights reserved.

It is not legal to reproduce, duplicate, or transmit any part of this document in either electronic means or in printed format. Recording of this publication is strictly prohibited and any storage of this document is not allowed unless with written permission from the publisher except for the use of brief quotations in a book review.

❀ Created with Vellum

CONTENTS

Author's Note: 1	1
Introduction	3
1. Learn the Letters of Alphabet in German	7
2. Learn Numbers in German	14
3. Learn Days of the Week in German	25
4. Learn Months Of The Year And Seasons In German	33
5. Learn Objects In The House In German	40
6. Learn Clothing Types In German	47
Author's Notes: 2	57
7. Learn Animals in German	59
8. Learn Emotions in German	64
9. Learn Different Foods in German	70
10. Learn Useful words for School in German	80
11. Learn Members of the Family in German	86
12. Learn Objects in Space and Compass Points in German	90
13. Learn Colors in German	93
14. Learn Conversation Starters in German	96
Author's Note: 3	100

AUTHOR'S NOTE: 1

Hey Language Learner, It's Pro Language Learning,

Before we start, I want to tell you about an exclusive offer just for readers of this book.

When learning any language, the time it takes to go from complete beginner to the level of a native speaker can sometimes take you a whole lifetime.

Quite painful to hear, right?

It would be but, luckily for you, I have partnered up with Audio Elevate who are giving away their award-winning book called Master Any Language that will give you all of the step-by-step strategies and fundamentals to learn any language in just a month!

Best thing about this exclusive offer is it is 100 percent FREE, no-strings-attached.

All you need to do to claim your FREE copy of Master

Any Language is either click below or type in on your search browsers URL: free.audioelevate.com

Once you are on the web page, fill out the required information that Audio Elevate asks for; this should only take less than 1 minute of your time. Then, straight-away you will receive in your email inbox the life changing book that has helped thousands of people around the world.

Before reading any further, please do this NOW as I may refer back to some of the chapters throughout this book!

INTRODUCTION

Do you think learning German is hard? Most people believe that learning German is very difficult. That's not the case. In fact, German is one of the easiest languages to learn. It is all in the mind. Learning anything new is always difficult at first. But, it becomes easier and easier once you have the momentum going. You only need to develop the right attitude and use the right tools.

The German language is the sister to English. Most German words sound like English and some words mean the same in both languages. Do you know that? To make it easier, the words in German are pronounced the same way they are spelled. There are no silent letters like there often are in English. Let's take for example the word *spielen*. What does it sound like? It sounds like spilling in English right? It means to play. What about *haus*? What does it sound like? To me, it sounds like the word *house*. And yes, it does mean a house. Very simple right? I guess you can now see how easy the language really is.

Before we dive into German, let us take a look at the differences and similarities that exist between the German language and English.

SIMILARITIES BETWEEN GERMAN AND ENGLISH

- They both use the 26 standard Latin alphabet letters.
- Both languages use Arabic numbering systems.
- They both have tense and follow the same grammatical rule of changing the verbs based on their tense ('drink' – 'drank' – 'drunk' in English and, 'trinkt' – 'trank' – 'getrunken' in German).
- Sentences in both languages follow the Subject-Verb word order.
- In both languages, the direct object always comes after the indirect object.

DIFFERENCES BETWEEN GERMAN AND ENGLISH

- German words do not have silent letters. Every letter you see has a sound and must be pronounced.

- The articles in German take three genders: 'der' is a definite article that takes nouns with the masculine gender; 'die' takes feminine-gendered and plural words; and 'das' takes words that are neuter. To compare, English uses 'a' and 'an' as indefinite articles and 'the' as the only definite article.
- All nouns in German are capitalized unlike English where we capitalize only the proper nouns.
- German has additional letters to the 26 standard alphabet letters: the umlauted vowels and a unique consonant.
- German has more than three different words for "you," while English has only one.
- In German, the order of the words in a sentence are slightly different. Sometimes, the verb appears last in a sentence.

TEACHING GERMAN TO CHILDREN

Younger kids learn foreign languages like German faster than older children, especially those between the ages of three and eight years. Children under the age of six years find learning a second language as easy as learning their mother tongue. This doesn't mean that it is naturally impossible for adults to learn a second language faster. It is equally possible. The difference that brings faster results in children is that most children at the age of six are enthusiastic and highly motivated to learn a new language.

They learn the language through German songs, nursery German rhymes, games and reading and telling German stories. Children never get bothered with wrong grammar and pronunciation. They keep working on getting it right without worry. Children always develop their grammatical skills subconsciously and quickly pick up an accent of another language.

Almost all children have a gift for languages, and they can easily learn German. Teaching them a new language, however, requires a lot of patience in addition to the right tools.

REASONS FOR LEARNING GERMAN

- To communicate effectively with native German-speakers, friends and family members.
- To increase your chances of securing jobs and careers in other parts of the world (Germany is one of the biggest economies in the world).
- To read the classics of German literature.
- To embrace the German culture.
- To carry out business with the German speaking territories.
- To break language barriers when touring the heart of Europe or any nation where German is spoken.

1

LEARN THE LETTERS OF ALPHABET IN GERMAN

Most non-German speakers perceive German as a rough sounding language. This may be partly due to certain German alphabet sounds and diphthongs that are more guttural in their pronunciation. Learning the German alphabet and the letters' pronunciation can be intimidating to neophytes. Once familiar with German's different sounds, everything falls in place and a kind of poetic magic unravels.

Just like English, German uses alphabetic letters in its language. In addition to the 26 standard alphabet letters, German contains the extra letters ä, ö, ü and ß. Each German letter has both uppercase and lowercase versions except the ß.

To grasp the letters of the alphabet in German, learn the alphabet characters and their respective pronunciations first. If possible, get yourself an audio version of a German dictionary.

It also helps to have a recording of the letters being spoken so that you can learn them systematically and slowly.

You can have your friends test you by making you spell out German words for them letter by letter. By doing so, they are able to judge your pronunciation and knowledge of the individual letters. German language games can also do you good. Both children and adults can learn German alphabet through playing games.

THE GERMAN ALPHABET'S SPECIAL CHARACTERISTICS

- Comprises a total of 30 letters: the standard 26 letters and the additional 4 unique letters.
- The Umlauted vowels (ä, ö, ü) and the unique consonant (ß) form the extra 4 letters.
- The pronunciation of some of its letters do not exist in the English language.
- Several letters are pronounced more from the back of the throat: g, ch, r (though in Austria the r is trilled).
- The German alphabet W sounds like the English alphabet V.
- The V in German sounds like the F in English.
- In most cases, when you place an S at the beginning of a word followed by a vowel, it sounds like the Z in English.

- The letter ß will never appear at the beginning of a word.
- The letter ß is not used in any other language.
- The letter ß does not have an uppercase or lowercase version.
- When spelling words on the phone or in radio, German has its own phonetic spelling code used to prevent misunderstanding.

THE GERMAN ALPHABET TABLE

The German Alphabet (Das Deutsche Alphabet)						
A a ah	Ä ä ah Umlaut	B b beh	ß esszett	C c tseh	D d deh
E e eh	F f eff	G g geh	H h ha	I i ee	J j yot
K k kah	L l ell	M m emm	N n enn	O o oh	Ö ö oh Umlaut
P p pee	Q q kuh	R r err	S s ess	T t teh	U u uh
Ü ü uh Umlaut	V v fow	W w veh	X x iks/ix	Y y upsilon	Z z tsett

THE GERMAN ALPHABET (DAS DEUTSCHE ALPHABET)

The German Alphabet (Das Deutsche Alphabet)

A a ah	Ä ä ah Umlaut	B b beh	ß esszett	C c tseh	D d deh
E e eh	F f eff	G g geh	H h ha	I i ee	J j yot
K k kah	L l ell	M m emm	N n enn	O o oh	Ö ö oh Umlaut
P p pee	Q q kuh	R r err	S s ess	T t teh	U u uh
Ü ü uh Umlaut	V v fow	W w veh	X x iks/ix	Y y upsilon	Z z tsett

THE GERMAN ALPHABET LETTERS, THEIR SOUNDS AND EXAMPLES

Ä ä	e	Ähnlich	Similar
ß	s	Heiß	Hot
B b	Beh	der Bruder	Brother
C c	tseh	der Chor	The choir
D d	deh	Dienstag	Tuesday
E e	eh	Essen	To eat
F f	eff	der Freund	Friend
G g	gay	Gut	Good
H h	ha	der Hammer	Hammer
I i	ee	der Igel	Porcupine
J j	yot	das Jahr	Year
K k	kah	das Kamel	Camel
L l	ell	das Land	Land
M m	em	der Mann	Man

Letter	Sound	*Beispiele*/Examples	English
N n	en	Nicht	Not
O o	oh	Ostern	Easter
Ö ö	i	Österreich	Austria
P p	pay	die Polizei	Police
Q q	koo	das Quadrat	Square
R r	err	der Rücken	The Black
S s	ess	Schön	Nice
T t	tay	der Tyrann	Tyrant
U u	uh	die Universität	University
Ü ü	'ui'	Über	Over
V v	fow	der Vogel	Bird
W w	vay	die Wange	Cheek
X x	ix	das Xylophon	Noun
Y y	upsilon	der Yeti	the snowman
Z z	tset	die Zeitung	Newspaper

2

LEARN NUMBERS IN GERMAN

German numbers form part of the language family tree's branch known as Germanic. The same branch consists of other languages like English, Dutch and Swedish. That's why there are a lot of similarities in the spelling and pronunciation of numbers in these languages. Take for example, the number 6 (six): in German it's spelled and pronounced 'sechs,' in Dutch 'zes,' Swedish 'sex' and both Norwegian and Danish spell it as 'seks.' Let's now learn more about German numbers.

CARDINAL NUMBERS / KARDINAL ZAHLEN

German Numbers 0 -9

These numbers don't have rules, therefore they don't follow any pattern. It is very important to recall these patterns as they occur in one form or another in other numbers while counting. For example, in English we can see the patterns in the way "**nine**" is placed in "**nine**teen," "Twenty-**nine**," "**nine**ty" and "**nine** hundred." The same pattern can be seen for *neun* ("nine") in German: "**Neun**zehn," "neunundzwanzig," "**neun**zig" and "**neun**hundert."

Number	German	Prononciation	English
0	null	(nul)	zero
1	eins	(ighnss)	one
2	zwei	(tsvigh)	two
3	drei	(drigh)	three
4	vier	(feer)	four
5	fünf	(fuunf)	five
6	sechs	(zekhs)	six
7	sieben	(ZEE-ben)	seven
8	acht	(ahkht)	eight
9	neun	(noyn)	nine

German Numbers 11 – 19

In this set of numbers, only *Elf* ("eleven") and *zwölf* ("twelve") lack a pattern. The remaining numbers: thirteen to nineteen, you only add the word "zehn" at the end of the first four letters for the numbers three up to nine.

Number	German	Pronunciation	English
11	elf	elf	eleven
12	zwölf	tswoolf	twelve
13	dreizehn	DRIGH-tsayn	thirteen
14	vierzehn	FEER-tsayn	fourteen
15	fünfzehn	FUUNF-tsayn	fifteen
16	sechzehn	ZEKH-tsayn	sixteen
17	siebzehn	ZEEP-tsayn	seventeen
18	achtzehn	AHKH-tsayn	Eighteen
19	neunzehn	NOYN-tsayn	nineteen

German Numbers 21 – 29

Normally, in English, numbers larger than twenty are said starting with the largest number followed by the smallest number. In English, you would say '21' as 'twenty-one.' In German, it is the other way round: you start with the smallest letter followed by the largest. Using the same example, you would say 'one and twenty' or 'einundzwanzig.' All of these numbers in German follow the number-swapping rule. It is regular across all the numbers above twenty including the 31 - 39, 41 - 49, 51 - 52, etc.

Number	German	Pronunciation	English
21	einundzwanzig	(IGHN-oont-tsvahn-tsikh)	Twenty one
22	zweiundzwanzig	(TSVIGH-oont-tsvahn-tsikh)	twenty two
23	dreiundzwanzig	(DRIGH-oont-tsvahn-tsikh)	twenty three
24	vierundzwanzig	(FEER-oont-tsvahn-tsikh)	Twenty four
25	fünfundzwanzig	(FUUNF-oont-tsvahn-tsikh)	twenty five
26	schesundzwanzig	(ZEKHS-oont-tsvahn-tsikh)	twenty six
27	siebenundzwanzig	(ZEE-ben-oont-tsvahn-tsikh)	twenty seven
28	achtundzwanzig	(AHKH-oont-tsvahn-tsikh)	twenty eight
29	neunundzwanzig	(NOYN-oont-tsvahn-tsikh)	Twenty nine

German for the Multiples of 10

In this set of numbers, only *zehn* ("ten") and *zwanzig* ("twenty") and dreißig ('thirty') are exceptional. The rest follow a pattern. From forty to ninety, you only need to add the word "zig" at the end of the first four letters for the numbers from four to nine.

Number	German	Pronunciation	English
10	zehn	(tsayn)	ten
20	zwanzig	(TSVAHN-tsikh)	twenty
30	dreißig	(DRIGH-sikh)	thirty
40	vierzig	(FEER-tsikh)	fourty
50	fünfzig	(FUUNF-tsikh)	fifty
60s	echzig	(ZEKH-tsikh)	sixty
70	siebzig	(ZEEP-tsikh)	seventy
80	achtzig	(AHKH-tsikh)	eighty
90	neunzig	(NOYN-tsikh)	ninety

German Numbers: Counting Hundreds (100 – 900)

The pattern followed when counting hundreds in German is exactly the same as in English. You simply add the word "hundert" (hundred) at the end of the numbers from one to nine (1-9). Here is how it is done:

Number	German	Pronunciation	English
100	einhundert	(IGHN-hoon-dert)	one hundred
200	zweihundert	(TSVIGH-hoon-dert)	two hundred
300	dreihundert	(DRIGH-hoon-dert)	Three hundred
400	Vierhundert	(FEER-hoon-dert)	four hundred
500	Fünfhundert	(FUUNF-hoon-dert)	Five hundred
600	Sechshundert	(ZEKH-hoon-dert)	six hundred
700	Siebenhundert	(ZEEP-hoon-dert)	seven hundred
800	Achthundert	(AHKH-hoon-dert)	Eight hundred
900	Neunhundert	(NOYN-hoon-dert)	nine hundred

Counting 1000 to 10000 in German

You don't need to remember much when counting these numbers in German. It is similar to English. You just apply the same rule used in the 100's. Simply add the word "tausend" (thousand) at the end of the numbers one to ten.

Number	German	Pronunciation	English
1000	Eintausend	(IGHN-TOW-zent)	One thousand
2000	Zweitausend	(TSVIGH-tow-zent)	two thousand
3000	Dreitausend	(DRIGH-tow-zent)	three thousand
4000	Viertausend	(FEER-tow-zent)	four thousand
5000	Fünftausend	(FUUNF-tow-zent)	five thousand
6000	Sechstausend	(ZEKH-tow-zent)	six thousand
7000	Siebentausend	(ZEEP-tow-zent)	Seven thousand
8000	Achttausend	(AHKH-tow-zent)	eight thousand
9000	Neuntausend	(NOYN-tow-zent)	nine thousand
10000	Zehntausend	(TSAYN-tow-zent)	ten thousand

German Numbers: Million, Billion and Trillion

Number	German	Pronunciation	English
1,000,000	eine Million	(igh-nuh mill-YOHN)	One Million
1,000,000,000	eine Milliarde	(igh-nuh mill-YAR-duh)	One Billion
1,000,000,000,000	eine Billion	(igh-nuh bill-YOHN)	One Trillion

ORDINAL NUMBERS / ORDNUNGSZAHLEN

Short Form

Short Form	German	English
1st	erste	first
2nd	zweite	second
3rd	dritte	third
4th	vierte	fourth
5th	fünfte	fifth
6th	sechste	sixth
7th	siebte	seventh
8th	achte	eighth
9th	neunte	ninth
10th	zehnte	tenth
11th	elfte	eleventh
12th	zwölfte	twelfth
13th	dreizehnte	thirteenth
14th	vierzehnte	fourteenth
15th	fünfzehnte	fifteenth
16th	sechzehnte	sixteenth

Short Form	German	English
17th	siebzehnte	seventeenth
18th	achtzehnte	eighteenth
19th	neunzehnte	nineteenth
20th	zwanzigste	twentieth
21st	einundzwanzigste	twenty-first
22nd	zweiundzwanzigste	twenty-second
23rd	dreiundzwanzigste	twenty-third
30th	dreißigste	thirtieth
31st	einunddreißigste	thirty-first
40th	vierzigste	fortieth
50th	fünfzigste	fiftieth
60th	sechzigste	sixtieth
70th	siebzigste	seventieth
80th	achtzigste	eightieth
90th	neunzigste	ninetieth
100th	hundertste	hundredth

Repetition

German	Pronunciation	English Translation
einmal	(*ighnss maal*)	Once
zweimal	(*tsvigh maal*)	twice
drei Mal	(*drigh maal*)	three times
vier Mal	(*feer maal*)	four times
fünf Mal	(*fuunf maal*)	five times
sechs Mal	(*zekhs maal*)	six times
sieben mal	(*ZEE-ben maal*)	seven times
acht Mal	(*ahkht maal*)	eight times
neun Mal	(*noyn maal*)	nine times
zehn Mal	(*tsayn maal*)	ten times
elf Mal	(*elf maal*)	eleven times
zwölf Mal	*tsvoolf maal*	twelve times
dreizehn Mal	*DRIGH-tsayn maal*	thirteen times
vierzehn Mal	*FEER-tsayn maal*	fourteen times

German	Pronunciation	English Translation
fünfzehn Mal	FUUNF-tsayn maal	fifteen times
sechzehn Mal	ZEKH-tsayn maal	sixteen times
siebzehn Mal	ZEEP-tsayn maal	seventeen times
achtzehn Mal	AHKH-tsayn maal	eighteen times
neunzehn Mal	NOYN-tsayn maal	nineteen times
einundzwanzig Mal	(IGHN-oont-tsvahn-tsikh maal)	Twenty one
zweiundzwanzig Mal	(TSVIGH-oont-tsvahn-tsikh maal)	twenty two
dreiundzwanzig Mal	(DRIGH-oont-tsvahn-tsikh maal)	twenty three
vierundzwanzig Mal	(FEER-oont-tsvahn-tsikh maal)	Twenty four
fünfundzwanzig Mal	(FUUNF-oont-tsvahn-tsikh maal)	twenty five
schesundzwanzig Mal	(ZEKHS-oont-tsvahn-tsikh maal)	twenty six
siebenundzwanzig Mal	(ZEE-ben-oont-tsvahn-tsikh maal)	twenty seven
achtundzwanzig Mal	(AHKH-oont-tsvahn-tsikh maal)	twenty eight
neunundzwanzig Mal	(NOYN-oont-tsvahn-tsikh maal)	Twenty nine

3

LEARN DAYS OF THE WEEK IN GERMAN

When learning any second language, the days of the week are probably among the first basics to learn and master. The days of the week in German is one of the best starting points for your journey to German fluency.

Days of the Week / Tage der Woche

English	German
What day is it today?	*Welcher Tag ist heute?*
Monday (moon day)	Montag (Mond-Tag)
Tuesday (Týr's day)	Dienstag (Týr's Tag)
Wednesday (mid-week)	Mittwoch
Thursday (thunder's day)	Donnerstag
Friday (Frige's day)	Freitag (Freya-Tag)
Saturday (Sabbath day)	Samstag
Sunday (sun day)	Sonntag (Sonne-Tag)

You must have heard of "Guten Tag" which means, "Good day." Every day of the week in German ends in *tag*, apart from Wednesday. You can now relate the meaning of Guten tag with this. *Tag* means *day*.

Montag (Monday) in German is derived from the German word Mond which means *moon*. Therefore, in German, Monday is moon day.

Dienstag (Tuesday) is connected to Týr, an old Germanic god. Dienstag was considered Týr's day. Sounds like Tuesday and that's where English got the name.

Mittwoch, or Wednesday, simply means mid-week. It is the only day of the week in German that lacks the *tag* at the end.

In German, Donnerstag (Thursday) literally refers to "thunder's day." Originally, it was named after Thor - a Norse god who was famously known as Donar by the German speaking cultures. That's where Donnerstag was derived from.

Freitag (Friday) comes from goddess Frige.

Samstag in German is Saturday in English and comes from the Greek older word sabbaton which is closely related to Sabbath.

Lastly, Sonntag (Sunday) was derived from a German word Sonne meaning sun. Therefore, Sonntag literally means "sun day." Thus the word Sunday in English. You can see how German and English are related.

USING GERMAN DAYS OF THE WEEK

Basic Rules

1. In German, Montag or 'Monday' is the first day of the week. As you speak the language, make sure that you understand the order of the days clearly. Some places refer to Sunday as the first day of the week.

2. The days of the week in German are usually capitalized. There is one exception, however: in situations where you want to express that something happens on a particular day every week. In such a case, you don't capitalize the first letter of the day as with many German nouns and you simply add an 's' to make it plural.

English	German
On Mondays	montags
On Tuesdays	dienstags
On Wednesdays	mittwochs
On Thursdays	donnerstags
On Fridays	freitags
On Saturdays	samstags
On Sundays	sonntags

Examples:

German	English
Ich gehe montags in die Schule	I go to school on Mondays
Ich gehe freitags in die Turnhalle	I go to the gym on Fridays
Ich gehe sonntags in die Kirche	I go to church on Sundays
Samtags schwimme ich	I swim on Saturdays
Er trifft seine Eltern dientags an.	He meets his parents on Tuesdays
Wir spielen mittwochs	We play on Wednesdays

3. All German nouns have gender and the days of the week fall under masculine. Therefore, they take masculine articles **der** (the) and **ein** (a).

German	English
der Montag	the Monday
der Dienstag	the Tuesday
der Mittwoch	the Wednesday
der Donnerstag	the Thursday
der Freitag	the Friday
der Samstag	the Saturday
der Sonntag	the Sunday

With ein (a) article

English	German
a Monday	ein Montag
a Tuesday	ein Dienstag
a Wednesday	ein Mittwoch
a Thursday	ein Donnerstag
a Friday	ein Freitag
a Saturday	ein Samstag
a Sunday	ein Sonntag

4. German *am* (English *on*) is used to indicate that something is happening on a particular day.

German	English
am Montag	on Monday
am Dienstag	on Tuesday
am Mittwoch	on Wednesday
am Donnerstag	on Thursday
am Freitag	on Friday
am Samstag	on Saturday
am Sonntag	on Sunday

Examples:

English	German
I will go to church on Sunday	Ich werde am Sonntag in die Kirche gehen
I will go to the gym on Friday	Ich werde am Freitag in die Turnhalle gehen
I will go to school on Monday	Ich werde am Montag in die Schule gehen

5. To denote 'from ……. to…', use "von … bis …"

Examples

German	English
Von Montag bis Dienstag ....From Monday to Tuesday
Von Mittwoch bis Donnerstag............. From Wednesday to Thursday
Von Freitag bis Samstag .... From Friday to Saturday
Von Sonntag bis Freitag .... From Sunday to Friday
Von Montag bis Montag .... From Monday to Monday

6. There are abbreviations for the German days of the week just like in English. Infact, it is very easy to abbreviate German days of the week. You just pick the first two letters.

English	German
Monday (Mon.) .... Montag (Mo)
Tuesday (Tue.) .... Dienstag (Di.)
Wednesday (Wed.) .... Mittwoch (Mi.)
Thursday (Thur.) .... Donnerstag (Do.)
Friday (Fri.) ....Freitag (Fr.)
Saturday (Sat.) ....Samstag (Sa.)
Sunday (Sun.) .... Sonntag (So.)

7. If you want to say that something happens on each specific day in a week repetitively, you use 'every' which is 'jeden' in German.

English	German
every Monday	jeden Montag
every Tuesday	jeden Dienstag
every Wednesday	jeden Mittwoch
every Thursday	jeden Donnerstag
every Friday	jeden Freitag
every Saturday	jeden Samstag
every Sunday	jeden Sonntag

Examples:

English	German
I go to church every Sunday	Ich gehe jeden Sonntag in die Kirche
I go to school every Monday	Ich gehe jeden Montag in die Schule
I go to the gym every Friday	Ich gehe jeden freitag in die Turnhalle

4

LEARN MONTHS OF THE YEAR AND SEASONS IN GERMAN

Learning the months of the year is fundamental to any language. The months of the year are part of basic vocabulary that are mentioned frequently in any language.

When learning the German language, you should master the calendar and how to communicate about it. This is a very important elementary milestone in learning how to communicate in German. It enables you to express dates correctly and talk about events and when they happened or will happen without fumbling.

English speakers and other languages related to German might be relieved to see that the names of the months in German look similar to what they already know, but it is very important to know the right spelling and pronunciation in German. Here is a list of the months of the year in German and how they are pronounced.

MONTHS OF THE YEAR / MONATEN DES JAHRES

English	German	Pronunciation in German
January	Januar	*yah-noo-ahr*
February	Februar	*fay-broo-ahr*
March	März	*mehrts*
April	April	*ah-pril*
May	Mai	*my*
June	Juni	*yoo-nee*
July	Juli	*yoo-lee*
August	August	*ow-goost*
September	September	*zehp-tehm-ber*
October	Oktober	*ok-toh-ber*
November	November	*no-vehm-ber*
December	Dezember	*deh-tsem-ber* 4

Just like in English, the months of the year in German can be abbreviated or rather written in short forms. For you to do that, it is very simple: just pick the first 3 letters of the month. Here is how they are written:

Januar	Jan
Februar	Feb
März	Mär
Apri	Apr
Mai	Mai
Juni	Jun
Juli	Jul
August	Aug
September	Sep
Oktober	Okt
November	Nov
Dezember	Dez

All nouns in German have gender, months of the year being a group of nouns that fall under masculine, they use the article 'der' to replace the English definite article "the". Here is how they should be written:

German	English
der Januar	the January
der Februar	the February
der März	the March
der April	the April
der Mai	the May
der Juni	the June
der Juli	the July
der August	the August
der September	the September
der Oktober	the October
der November	the November
der Dezember	the December

To say *in* a particular month in German, use *im*.

Examples:

German	English
im Januar	in January
im Februar	in February
im März	in March
im April	in April
im Mai	in May
im Juni	in June
im Juli	in July
im August	in August
im September	in September
im Oktober	in October
im November	in November
im Dezember	in December

Examples in a sentence:

German	English
Wann hast du Geburtstag?	When is your birthday?
Mein Hochzeitstag ist im Oktober.	My wedding day is in October
Wann hast du Abschluss?	When is your graduation?
Mein Abschluss ist im Dezember	My graduation is in December
Wann hat Jane Geburtstag?	When is Jane's birthday?
Janes Geburtstag ist im Oktober	Jane's birthday is in October

Seasons of the Year in German

English	German
Spring	der Frühling
Summer	der Sommer
autumn	der Herbst
winter	der Winter

To express that something happened or happens in a specific season we use *im*.

German	English
im Frühling	in spring
im Sommer	in summer
im Winter	in winter
im Herbst	in autumn

Examples in Sentences:

German	English
Es schneit im Winter	It snows in winter
Es ist immer heiß im Sommer	It is always hot in summer
Blätter fallen im Herbst von den Bäumen	Leaves fall off the trees in autumn
Die Blätter wachsen im Frühling	Leaves grow in spring

5

LEARN OBJECTS IN THE HOUSE IN GERMAN

Rooms in an Apartment or House /die Zimmer in einem Haus oder in einer Wohnung

English	Deutsch
Room	**das Zimmer**
storage room	der Abstellraum
office, workroom	das Arbeitszimmer
bathroom, bath	das Badezimmer, das Bad
balcony	der Balkon
office	das Büro
attic	der Dachboden
dining room	das Esszimmer
hall, entry	der Flur
garage	die Garage
cellar, basement	der Keller
children's room	das Kinderzimmer
shower	die Dusche
kitchen	die Küche
dresser	die Kommode
bedroom	das Schlafzimmer
toilet (room)	die Toilette/das WC
laundry room	die Waschküche
closet	der (Kleider)schrank
living room	das Wohnzimmer

Parts of an Apartment / House

English	German
window	das Fenster
ground floor	das Erdgeschoss
1st floor/storey	der erste Stock
floor/ground	der Boden
stairs/steps	die Treppen
mirror	der Spiegel
Floor	der Boden
hallway/corridor	der Flur
shelf	das Regal
roof	das Dach
bathroom sink	das Waschbecken
drawer	die Schublade
bookcase	das Bücherregal
bathtub	die Badewanne
blanket, ceiling	die Decke
door	die Tür
wall	die Wand
lawn	der Rasen
garden, yard	der Garten

Furniture / die Möbel

English	Deutsch	Plural
Clothes rack	der Garderobenständer	die Garderobenständer
Bed	das Bett	die Betten
Bookcase	das Bücherregal	die Bücherregale
Double bed	das Doppelbett	die Doppelbetten
Single Bed	das Einzelbett	die Einzelbetten
Cot	das Kinderbett	die Kinderbetten
shoe cabinet	das Schuhregal	die Schuhregale
Sofa	das Sofa	die Sofas
Shelf	das Wandregal	die Wandregale
Stool	der Hocker	die Hocker
Room divider	der Japanische Wandschirm	die Japanische Wandschirme
Nightstand	der Nachttisch	die Nachttische
Umbrella stand	der Schirmständer	die Schirmständer
Cabinet /Cupboard	der Schrank	die Schränke
Armchair	der Sessel	die Sessel
Mirror	der Spiegel	die Spiegel
Chair	der Stuhl	die Stühle
Table	der Tisch	die Tische
Laundry basket	der Wäschekorb	die Wäschekörbe
Chest of drawers	die Kommode	die Kommoden
Trunk	die Truhe	die Truhen
Showcase	die Vitrine	die Vitrinen
Moses basket	die Wiege	die Wiegen

Kitchen items

German	Pronunciation	English Translation
der Herd	(dehr HEHRD)	the stove
der Backofen	(dehr BAHK-oh-fehn)	the oven
die Dunstabzugshaube	(dee duhnst-ahb-zoogs-how-beh)	the exhaust hood
die Mikrowelle	(dee MEEK-roh-veh-leh)	the microwave
der Toaster	(dehr TOH-stehr)	the toaster
die Kaffeemaschine	(dee KAH-feh-mah-shee-neh)	the coffee machine
die Geschirrspülmaschine	(dee geh-SHIHR-shpül-mah-shee-neh)	the dishwasher
der Kühlschrank	(dehr KÜL-shrahnk)	the refrigerator
das Gefrierfach	(dahs geh-FREER-fahkh)	the freezer
die Küche	(dee KÜ-hehn)	the kitchen
der Küchentisch	(dehr KÜ-hehn-teesh)	the kitchen desk
der Küchenstuhl	(dehr KÜ-hehn-shtool)	the kitchen chair
der Mülleimer	(dehr MÜL-iy-mehr)	the trash bin
die Arbeitsplatte	(dee AHR-biyts-plah-teh)	the worktop (countertop)
das Spülbecken	(dahs SHPÜL-beh-kehn)	the kitchen sink
der Wasserhahn	(dehr VAH-sehr-hahn)	the water tap
das Geschirrspülmittel	(dahs geh-SHIHR-shpool-mih-tehl)	the dishwashing detergent
das Geschirrtuch	(dahs geh-SHIHR-tooh)	the dish cloth

German	Pronunciation	English Translation
der Küchenschrank	(dehr KÜ-hehn-shrahnk)	the kitchen cabinet
das Geschirr	(dahs geh-SHIHR)	the dishes
der Suppenteller	(dehr ZOO-pehn-teh-lehr)	the soup plate
das Glas	(dahs glahs)	the glass
die Tasse	(dee tahse)	the cups
der Teller	(dehr TEH-lehr)	the plates
der Hängeschrank	(dehr HÄN-geh-shrahnk)	the wall cabinet
der Topf	(dehr TOHPF)	the pot
die Pfanne	(dee PFAH-neh)	the pan
das Kochbuch	(dahs KOHKH-tooh)	the cookbook
das Handtuch	-	towel
die Geschirrspülmaschine	-	dishwasher
der Wasserhahn	-	faucet
der Papierkorb	-	wastebasket
das Besteck	-	silverware
das Spülbecken	-	kitchen sink
das Geschirr	-	dishes

Other Objects in the House

English	German
picture	das Bild
curtain	der Vorhang
clock	die Uhr
lamp	die Lampe
alarm clock	der Wecker
pillow	das Kopfkissen
vase	die Vase
rug	der Teppich
VCR	der Videorekorder
CD Player	der CD-Spieler
computer	der Computer
radio	das Radio
telephone	das Telefon
television	der Fernseher

6

LEARN CLOTHING TYPES IN GERMAN

Common Clothing

English	Plural	German	Plural
suit	suits	der Anzug	die Anzüge
Bermuda short	Bermuda shorts	die Bermuda kur	die Bermuda shorts
blouse	blouses	die Bluse	die Blusen
dress	dresses	das Kleid	die Kleider
chinos	chinos	die Chinohose	die Chinohosen
shirt	Shirts	das Hemd	die Hemden
pants	pants	die Hose	die Hosen
jacket	jackets	die Jacke	die Jacken
jeans	jeans	die Jeans	die Jeans
overalls	overalls	die Latzhose	die Latzhosen
leather pants,	Leather pants	die Lederhose	die Lederhosen
pullover	pullovers	der Pullover	die Pullover
skirt	skirts	der Rock	die Röcke
sweater	sweaters	der Sweater	die Sweater
sweatshirt	sweatshirts	das Sweatshirt	die Sweatshirts
top	tops	das Top	die Tops
t-shirt	t-shirts	das T-Shirt	die T-Shirts
vest	vests	die Weste	die Westen

Footwear (die Schuhe)

English	Plural	German	Plural
slipper	slippers	der Hausschuh	die Hausschuhe
sneaker	sneakers	der Turnschuh	die Turnshuhe
heel	heels	der Absatzschuh	die Absatzschuhe
sandal	sandals	die Sandale	die Sandalen
cleat	cleats	die Querleiste	die Querleisten
flip-flop	flip-flops	der Badelatsch	die Badelatschen
shoe	shoes	der Schuh	die Schuhe
clog	clogs	der Holzschuh	die Holzschuhe
boot	boots	der Stiefel	die Stiefel
loafer	loafers	der Halbschuh	die Halbschuhe
stiletto	stilettos	Der Stiletto	die Stilettos

Accessories (die Zubehöre)

English	Plural	German	Plural
necktie	neckties	der Binder	die Binder
shoelace	Shoelaces	die Schnürsenkel	die Schnürsenkel
earring	earings	der Ohrring	die Ohrringe
bow tie	Bow ties	die Fliege	die Fliegen
belt	belts	der Gürtel	die Gürtel
bracelet	braceletes	das Armband	die Armbander
glove	gloves	der Handschuh	die Handschuhe
hat	hats	der Hut	die Hüte
ring	rings	der Ring	die Ringe
tie	ties	die Krawatte	die Krawatten
turban	turbans	der Kopfbund	der Kopfbünde
cap	caps	die Mütze	die Mützen
necklace	necklaces	die Halskette	die Halsketten
scarf	scarfs	der Schal	die Schale
tie	ties	der Schlips	die Schlipse
baby blanket	Baby blankets	das Wickeltuch	die Wickeltücher
cape	capes	die Kappe	die Kappe

Underwear (die Unterwäsche)

English	Plural	German	Plural
boxer	boxers	die Boxershorts	die Boxershorts
bra	bras	der Büstenhalter	die Büstenhalter
panty	panties	der Schlüpfer	die Schlüpfer
socks	socks	die Socke	die Socken
stocking	stockings	der Strumpf	die Strümpfe
undershirt	undershirts	das Unterhemd	die Unterhemdem
underpants	underpants	die Unterhose	die Unterhosen
tight	tights	die Strumpfhose	die Strumpfhosen

Winter clothing (die Winterkleidung)

English	Plural	German	Plural
anorak	anoraks	der Anorak	die Anoraks
duffle coat	Duffle coats	der Dufflecoat	die Dufflecoats
overcoat	overcoats	der Mantel	die Mäntel
rain jacket	Rain jackets	der Regenmantel	die Regenmäntel

Bathing suits (die Badekleidung)

English	Plural	German	Plural
bathing suit	Bathing suits	der Badeanzug	die Badeanzüge
swimsuit	swimsuits	die Badehose	die Badehosen
bikini	bikinis	der Bikini	die Bikinis

Fabrics (der Stoff)

English	German
cotton	die Baumwolle
chemical fiber	die Chemiefaser
corduroy	der Cord
patent leather	der Lack
silk	die Seide
suede	das Wildleder
wool	die Wolle

Parts of clothing (die Kleidungsteile)

English	Plural	German	Plural
lining	linings	das Futter	die Futter
bib	bibs	der Latz	die Lätze
cuff	cuffs	die Manschette	die Manschetten
button hole	Button holes	die Schlitzloch	die Schlitzlöcher
pocket	pockets	die Tasche	die Taschen
hem	hems	der Überschlag	die Überschlage
V-neckline	V-necklines	der V-Ausschnitt	der V-Ausschnitte

Clothing characteristics

English	German
patterned	gemustert
single colored	Einfarbig
striped	gestreift
dotted	gepunktet
Checkered	kariert
Flowered	geblümt

Examples in sentences

English	German
She is in a striped shirt	Sie trägt ein gestreiftes Hemd
She is wearing a flowered dress	Sie trägt ein geblümtes Kleid
He is wearing a single colored shirt	Er trägt ein einfarbiges Hemd
He is in a patterned coat	Er trägt einen gemusterten Mantel
She is wearing a dotted dress	Sie trägt ein gepunktetes Kleid
They are all wearing checkered shirts	Sie tragen alle karierte Hamden

Some verbs that require dative objects can be used with clothing. They include:

English	German
To like	gefallen
To fit	passen
To look (good or bad)	stehen

Examples in a sentences:

English	German
The shoes fits him	Die Schuhe passen zu ihm
Do you like this dress?	Gefällt dir dieses Kleid?
The suit doesn't look good on me	Der Anzug steht mir nicht
That dress looks good on you!	Dieses Kleid steht dir sehr gut!

AUTHOR'S NOTES: 2

Hey Language Learner, it's Pro Language Learning,

As mentioned at the start of this book, you have an exclusive offer available to you for a short period of time.

In case you forgot to claim your 100 percent FREE, no strings attached, copy of Master Any Language by Audio Elevate, please make sure to do so NOW!

The reason for this is in the next coming chapters I will be discussing and referring back to parts of the book, which Audio Elevate has created for you to improve your fundamentals when learning a new language.

It will be pivotal to have this book available at all times as when learning a language, as it will help you learn in a quick and effective manner.

In case you forgot how to claim your FREE copy of

Master Any Language, either click below or type in on your search browsers URL: free.audioelevate.com

Remember, before reading any further, please do this NOW as I will refer back to parts of Master Any Language throughout this book!

LEARN ANIMALS IN GERMAN

Birds and animals make up an interesting category of words in German. You will find that many German words for animals and birds are similar in English. In German, however, all nouns have gender and these genders are represented by articles: der, das and die. That's why each word for animal or bird starts with an article that represents its gender followed by name. Also remember, all nouns in German start with a capital letter. Below is a list of words for animals and birds in German:

English	Plural	German	Plural
cat	cats	die Katze	die Katzen
rhino	rhinos	das Nashorn	die Nashörner
hippo	hippos	das Flusspferd	die Flusspferde
crocodile	crocodiles	das Krokodil	die Krokodile
rabbit	rabbits	das Kaninchen	die Kaninchen
camel	camels	das Kamel	die Kamele
chicken	chickens	das Hühnchen	die Hühnchen
chicken	chickens	das Huhn	die Hühner
pet	pets	das Haustier	die Haustiere
squirrel	squirrels	das Eichhörnchen	die Eichhörnchen
wolf	wolve	der Wolf	die Wölfe
whale	whales	der Wal	die Wale
bird	birds	der Vogel	die Vögel
tiger	tigers	der Tiger	die Tiger

English	Plural	German	Plural
scorpion	scorpions	der Skorpion	die Skorpione
swan	swans	der Schwan	die Schwäne
penguin	penguins	der Pinguin	die Pinguine
parrot	parrots	der Papagei	die Papageien
lion	lions	der Löwe	die Löwen
crab	crabs	der Krebs	die Krebben
beetle	beetles	der Käfer	die Käfer
hedgehog	hedgehogs	der Igel	die Igel
deer	deer	der Hirsch	viele Hirsche
hare	hares	der Hase	die Hasen
hamster	hamsters	der Hamster	die Hamster
shark	sharks	der Hai	die Haie
cock	cocks	der Hahn	die Hahne
fox	foxes	der Fuchs	die Füchse
frog	frogs	der Frosch	die Frösche

English	Plural	German	Plural
fish	fish	der Fisch	die Fisch
donkey	donkeys	der Esel	die Esel
elephant	elephants	der Elefant	die Elefanten
Gorilla	gorillas	der Gorilla	die Gorilla
polar bear	Polar bears	der Eisbär	die Eisbären
dolphin	dolphins	der Delfin	die Delfine
badger	badgers	der Dachs	die Dachs
bear	bears	der Bär	die Bären
monkey	monkeys	der Affe	die Affen
goat	goats	die Ziege	die Ziegen
pigeon	pigeons	die Taube	die Tauben
spider	spiders	die Spinne	die Spinnen
snake	snakes	die Schlange	die Schlangen
turtle	turtles	die Schildkröte	die Schildkröten
rat	rats	die Ratte	die Ratten
jellyfish	jellyfish	die Qualle	die Quallen

English	Plural	German	Plural
mouse	mice	die Maus	die Mäuse
cow	cows	die Kuh	die Kühe
shrimp	shrimps	die Krabbe	die Krabben
giraffe	giraffes	die Giraffe	die Giraffen
goose	geese	die Gans	die Gänse
bat	bats	die Fledermaus	die Fledermäuse
bull	bulls	der Bulle	die Bullen
owl	owls	die Eule	die Eulen
duck	ducks	die Ente	die Enten
eagle	eagles	der Adler	die Adler
zebra	zebras	das Zebra	die Zebras
alligator	alligators	das Alligator	die Alligatoren
pig	pigs	das Schwein	die Schweine
sheep	sheep	das Schaf	die Schafe
horse	horses	das Pferd	die Pferde
dog	dogs	der Hund	die Hunde

8

LEARN EMOTIONS IN GERMAN

We all experience feelings and emotions. It is therefore important to learn them in German to be able to express ourselves when we meet German native speakers. Here is a list of the German words for the most common emotions that most of us experience. Take a look!

English	German
Worried	besorgt
Amused	amüsiert
Tensed	angespannt
Apathetic	apathisch
Excited	aufgeregt
Depressed	bedrückt
Satisfied	befriedigt
Excited	begeistert
Offended	beleidigt
Sad	traurig
Embarrassed	peinlich
Afraid	ängstlich
Kind	Art
Happy	glücklich
Touched	berührt
Ashamed	beschämt
Concerned	beunruhigt
Moved	bewegt
Angry	böse
Thankful	dankbar
Jealous	eifersüchtig

English	German
Awed	eingeschüchtert
Lonely	einsam
Discouraged	entmutigt
Determined	entschlossen
Relaxed	entspannt
Disappointed	enttäuscht
Pleased	erfreut
Relieved	erleichtert
In love	verliebt
Exhausted	erschöpft
Frightened	erschreckt
Shocked	erschrocken
Impolite	unhöflich
Painful	empfindlich
Bored	gelangweilt
Tired	müde
Sensitive	Schmerzhaft
Undecided	unentschlossen
Unhappy	unglücklich

English	German
Restless	unruhig
Uncertain	unsicher
Discontented	unzufrieden
Scared	verängstigt
Upset	verärgert
Stunned	verblüfft
Delighted	erfreut
Amazed	erstaunt
Hesitant	zögernd
Wrathful	zornig
Pleased	zufrieden
Confident	zuversichtlich
Hatred	Hassen
Calm	ruhig
Surprised	überrascht.
Hopeless	hoffnungslos
Hopeful	hoffnungsvoll
Hungry	hungrig
Inspired	inspiriert
Interested	interessiert
Irritated	irritiert

Examples in sentences

English	German
I am annoyed	ich bin genervt
I am happy	ich bin glücklich
I am guilty	ich bin schuldig
I am nervous	ich bin nervös
I am optimistic	ich bin optimistisch
I am tired	ich bin müde
I am motivated	ich bin motiviert
I am bored	ich bin gelangweilt
I am frustrated	ich bin frustriert
I am lonely	ich bin einsam
She is irritated	Sie ist irritiert
She is unhappy	Sie ist unglücklich
She is restless	Sie ist unruhig
She is uncertain	Sie ist unsicher
She is discontented	Sie ist unzufrieden
She is scared	Sie ist verängstigt

English	German
She is upset	Sie ist verärgert
He is stunned	Er ist verblüfft
He is embarrassed	Er ist verlegen
He is vulnerable	Er ist verletzlich
He is hurt	Er ist verletzt
He is confused	Er ist verwirrt
We are in love	Wir sind verliebt
We are astonished	Wir sind verwundert
We are pleased	Wir sind zufrieden
We are hesitant	Wir sind zögernd
We are undecided	Wir sind unentschlossen
They are overwhelmed	Sie sind überwältigt
They are surprised	Sie sind überrascht
They are sad	Sie sind traurig
They are proud	Sie sind stolz
They are worriless	Sie sind sorgenfrei

9

LEARN DIFFERENT FOODS IN GERMAN

Imagine you are in Germany and you are starving. As you move around the city with your non-German speaking guardian or friend, your stomachs begin to growl. Everyone you meet on the street is busy and focused on minding their own business. You have been so busy using your brilliant brains to figure out where to go and what to buy and now it's time to attend to another important part of your bodies: your stomachs.

Before you begin to satisfy your hunger, you must know some German vocabulary for food and how to order whatever you want in German. It is therefore important to learn food vocabulary in German. By the end of this chapter, you will have some of these vocabularies on your fingertips.

English	German
Breakfast	Frühstück
Lunch	Mittagessen
Dinner	Abendessen
Coffee	der Kaffee
Fish	der Fisch
Milk	die Milch
Salad	der Salat
Beverage	der Getränk
Tea	der Tee
butter	die Butter
egg	das Ei
cheese	der Käse
ham	der Schinken
sausage	die Wurst
pork	das Schweinefleisch

English	German
beef	das Rindfleisch
chicken	das Hühnerfleisch
turkey	das Putenfleisch
Margarine	die Margarine
Yoghurt	der Joghurt
Cheese	der Käse
Salmon	der Lachs
Mustard	der Senf
Ketchup	das Ketchup
Gherkins	die Gurke
Beer	das Bier
Wine	der Wein
Water	das Wasser
Ham	der Schinken
French Fries	die Pommes Frites

Fruits / das Obst

fruit	plural	das Obst	plural
apple	apples	der Apfel	die Äpfel
pineapple	pineapples	die Ananas	die Ananasse
banana	bananas	die Banane	die Bananen
pear	pears	die Birne	die Birnen
strawberry	strawberries	die Erdbeere	die Erdbeeren
cherry	cherries	die Kirsche	die Kirschen
melon	melons	die Melone	die Melonen
orange	oranges	die Orange	die Orangen
peach	peaches	der Pfirsich	die Pfirsiche
watermelon	watermelons	die Wassermelone	die Wassermelonen
grape	grapes	die Weintraube	die Weintrauben
lemon	lemons	die Zitrone	die Zitronen
blackberry	Blackberries	die Brombeere	die Brombeeren
fig	figs	die Feige	die Feigen
pomegranate	pomegranates	der Granatapfel	die Granatäpfel
raspberry	raspberries	die Himbeere	die Himbeeren
kiwi	kiwis	die Kiwi	die Kiwis
coconut	coconuts	die Kokosnuss	die Kokosnüsse
plum	plums	die Zwetschge	die Zwetschgen

Vegetables / das Gemüse

English	Plural	German	Plural
Cauliflower	cauliflowers	der Blumenkohl	die Blumenkohle
Broccoli	broccolis	der Broccoli	die Broccoli
Celery	celeries	der echte Sellerie	die Sellerien
Spinach	spinach	der Gemüsespinat	die Gemüsespinat
Zucchini	Zucchinis	die Zucchini	die Zucchini
Lettuce	Lettuces	der Gartensalat	die Gartensalate
Garlic	Garlics	der Knoblauch	die Knoblauche
Pumpkin	Pumpkins	der Kürbis	die Kürbisse
Leek	Leeks	der Lauch	die Lauche
Corn	Corns	der Mais	die Maise
Chard	Chards	der Mangold	die Mangolde
Pepper	Pepper	der Paprika	die Paprikas
Cabbage	cabbages	der Kohl	die Kohle
Broad bean	Broad beans	die Ackerbohne	die Ackerbohnen
Eggplant	Eggplants	die Aubergine	die Auberginen
Pea	Peas	die Erbse	die Erbsen
Green bean	Green beans	die grüne Bohne	die grünen Bohnen
Cucumber	Cucumbers	die Gurke	die Gurken
Beetroot	Beetroots	die Rote Bete	die roten Beten
Tomato	Tomatoes	die Tomate	die Tomaten
Onion	onions	die Zwiebel	die Zwiebeln
Radish	Radishes	der Garten- Rettich	die Rettiche
Carrot	Carrots	die Karotte	die Karotten
Potato	Potatoes	die Kartoffel	die Kartoffeln
Turnip	Turnips	die Rübe	die Rüben

Spices

You may also be interested in cooking or eager to know the type of spices used to prepare the food you are eating or want to order. Here to help is a list of spices in German:

English	German
Nutmeg	die Muskatnuss
Vanilla	die Vanille
Basil	das Basilikum
Chervil	der Echte Kerbel
Coriander	der Echte Koriander
Laurel	der Echte Lorbeer
Tarragon	der Estragon
Fennel	der Fenchel
Oregano	der Oregano
Rosemary	der Rosmarin
Salvia	der Salbei
Thymus	der Thymian
Mentha	die Minze
Parsley	die Petersilie
Lemon balm	die Zitronenmelisse

Desserts

Do you love candies? What about sweets? I know you definitely love them! Do you know what they are called in German? I thought you should know. Below is a number of desserts and what they are called in German.

English	Plural	German	Plural
chocolate	Chocolates	die Schokolade	die Schokladen
candy	candies	das Bonbon	die Bonbons
ice cream	Ice creams	die Eiscreme	die Eiscremes
cookie	cookies	der Keks	die Kekse
cake	cakes	der Kuchen	die Kuchen
Raisin	raisins	die Rosine	die Rosinen

Describing Food (Essen Beschreiben)

You may want to describe the meal or food you ate. Here is a list of adjectives for describing food. Remember their endings change when used in a sentence.

English	German	Examples of phrases	Phrases in German
salty	salzig	Salty rice	Salziger Reis
sour	sauer	Sour milk	Saure Milch
delicious	delikat	Delicious meal	Leckeres Essen
warm	warm	Warm milk	Warm Milch
bitter	bitter	Bitter herbs	Bittere Kräuter
cold	kalt	Cold water	Kaltes Water
crispy	knusprig	Crispy potatoes	Knusprige Kartoffeln
sweet	Süß	Sweet oranges	Süße Orangen
tender	zart	Tender meat	Zartes Fleisch
fresh	frisch	Fresh juice	Frischer Saft
tasteless	Geschmacklos	Tasteless vegetables	Geschmackloses Gemüse
light	leicht	Light breakfast	Leichtes Frühstück
raw	roh	Raw meat	Rohes Fleisch
juicy	saftig	Juicy mangoes	Saftige Mangoes
strongly spiced	stark gewürzt	Strongly spiced food	Start gewürztes Essen
tasty	lecker	Tasty avocados	Leckere Avocados
delicious	köstlich	Delicious apples	Leckere Äpfel
heavy	schwer	Heavy lunch	Schweres Mittagessen
unusual, offbeat	Ungewöhnlich	Unusual meal	Ungewöhnlicher Mahlzeit
spicy	scharf	Spicy food	Scharfes Essen
creamy	cremig	Creamy tomato soup	Cremig Tomatensuppe
exquisite	ausgezeichnet	Exquisite cake	Exquisite Kuchen
Crunchy	knackig	Crunchy Granola	Knuspriges Müsli
hot	Heiß	Hot soup	Heiße Suppe
mild	mild	Mild spices	Milde Gewürze
bland	fade	Bland sauce	Milde Sauce
disgusting	ekelhaft	Disgusting stew	Widerlicher Eintopf

Verbs used in Food Preparation

English	German
to bake	bachen
to boil	kochen
to cook	kochen
to fry	braten
to grill	grillen
to heat	zu erhitzen
microwave	Microwelle
to poach	zu pochieren
to roast	braten
to steam	Zu dämpfen

Examples in sentences

Ich habe die Milch gekocht, bevor ich sie genommen habe.
I boiled the milk before taking it.
Wirst du ein paar Kuchen zu meinem Geburtstag backen?
Are you going to bake some cake for my birthday?

Wir werden zusammen kochen.
We are going to cook together.
Wirst du die Eier braten oder kochen?
Will you fry the eggs or boil them?
Kann ich ein gegrilltes Huhn haben?
Can I have a grilled chicken?
Hol mir geröstete Erdnüsse.
Get me roasted groundnuts.

LEARN USEFUL WORDS FOR SCHOOL IN GERMAN

Yes! We are in school now. Maybe you are in a school in a German speaking country or you are planning to visit or transfer into school in German. You are wondering how you will get along with others in classes and around the school compound; you need to learn the most commonly used vocabulary, in this case. Therefore, to help you, here is a list of school vocabulary in German.

Singular	Plural	Singular	Plural
Classroom	classrooms	das Klassenzimmer	die Klassenzimmer
Library	libraries	das Bibliothek	die Bibliotheken
Librarian (male)	librarians	der Bibliothekar	die Bibliothekare
Librarian (female)	librarians	die Bibliothekarin	die Bibliothekarinnen
Hall	halls	die Halle	die Hallen
Staffroom	staff rooms	das Lehrerzimmer	die Lehrerzimmere
Teacher (male)	teachers	der Lehrer	die Lehrere
Teacher (female)	teachers	die Lehrerin	die Lehrerinnen
cloakroom	cloakrooms	die Garderobe	die Garderoben
toilet	toilets	die Toillette	die Toilletten
laboratory	laboratories	das Labor	die Labore
workshop	workshops	die Werkstatt	die Wrestätten
sports field	sports fields	der Platz	die Plätze
headmaster	headmasters	der Schulleiter	die Schulleitere
headmistress	headmistresses	die Schulleiterin	die Schulleiterinnen
secretary (male)	secretaries	der Sekretär	die Sekretäre
Secretary (female)	secretaries	die Sekretärin	die Sekretärinnen
dining hall	dining halls	der Speisesaal	die Speisesäle
corridor	corridors	der Korridor	die Korridore
caretaker	caretakers	der Hausmeister	die Hausmeistere
school yard	school yards	der Schulhof	die Schulhöfe

Singular	Plural	Singular	Plural
Ballpoint pen	Ballpoint pens	der Kugelschreiber	die Kugelschreiber
fountain pen	Fountain pens	der Füller	die Füller
Pencil	Pencils	der Bleistift	die Bleistifte
Eraser	Erasers	das Radiergummi	die Radiergummis
Chalk	Chalks	die Kreide	die Kreide
Blackboard	Blackboards	die Tafel	die Tafeln
Paper	Papers	das Papier	die Papiere
Book	Books	das Buch	die Büch
Text book	Text books	das Lehrbuch	die Lehrbücher
Exercise book	Exercise books	das Heft	die Hefte
Calculator	Calculators	der Rechner	die Rechnere
Lesson	Lessons	die Stunde	die Stunden
Pupil (male)	Pupils	der Schüler	die Schülere
Pupil (female)	Pupils	die Schülerin	die Schülerinnen
Boarder	Boarders	der Pensionär	die Pensionäre
Bell	Bells	die Klingel	die Klingeln
Homework	Homework	die Hausaufgaben	die Hausaufgaben
Timetable	Timetables	der Stundenplan	die Stundenpläne
Semester	Semesters	das Semester	die Semester
Term	terms	das Trimester	die Trimester
Detention	detention	das Nachsitze	die Nachsitzen

Subjects learned in School

English	das Englisch
Mathematics	die Mathe
Physical Science	die Wissenschaft
Physics	die Physik
Chemistry	die Chemie
Biology	die Biologie
Woodwork	die Holzarbeit
Art	die Kunst
Computing (IT)	die Informatik
Music	die Musik
Geography	die Erdkunde
History	die Geschichte
Physical Education (PE)	der Sport
Religious Education (RE)	der Religionsunterricht

Sports and Games

Do you like playing? I bet the answer is Yes! I am sure you would love to learn some German words for different games and sports. Below is a list of vocabulary for sports and games in German.

German	English
Basketball (or Korbball)	Basketball
Fahrradfahren	Bike riding
Fußtball:	Soccer
Golf	golf
Handball	handball
Joggen	jogging
Karten	playing cards
Schach	chess
Schlittschuh laufen	ice skating
Schwimmen	swimming
Ski laufen	skiing
Tennis	Tennis
Tischtennis	Ping-Pong

Examples in sentences:

German	English Translation
Spielst du gerne Basketball?	Do you like playing Basketball?
Fahrst du gerne Fahrrad?	Do you like bike riding?
Ben spielt gut Fuftball	Ben plays soccer very well
Spielst du Golf? Es ist mein Lieblingssport	Do you play Golf? It is my favourite sport
Wirst du Handball spielen diese Saison?	Will you play handball this season
Wo gehst du joggen?	Where do you go jogging?
Die Jungen spielen im Unterricht Karten.	The boys are playing cards in class
Lindah spielt gem Schach	Lindah likes to play chess.
Wir werden morgen Eislaufen gehen	We will go ice skating tomorrow
Sie schwimmt gern	She likes swimming
Sie gehen Ski laufen	They are going skiing
Ich mag es, Tennis zu spielen	I like playing Tennis

LEARN MEMBERS OF THE FAMILY IN GERMAN

We all have family members and know what we call them in our first languages. Imagine you are in a German speaking nation or you come across a German native speaker who asks about your family member, will you be able to answer? It doesn't hurt to learn the family members in German. Take a look!

singular	plural	singular	Plural
mother	mothers	die Mutter	die Mütter
father	fathers	der Vater	die Väter
sister	sisters	die Schwester	die Schwestern
brother	brothers	der Bruder	die Brüder
wife	wives	die Ehefrau	die Ehefrauen
wife	wives	die Gattin	die Gattinnen
husband	husbands	der Ehemann	die Ehemänner
husband	husbands	der Gatte	die Gatten
daughter	daughters	die Tochter	die Töchter
son	sons	der Sohn	die Söhn

Grand parents

Singular	Plural	German	Plural
grandmother	grandmothers	die Großmutter	die Großmütter
grandfather	grandfathers	der Großvater	die Großväter
great-grandfather	great-grandfathers	der Urgroßvater	die Urgroßväte
great-grandmother	Great-grandmothers	die Urgroßmutter	die Urgroßmütter

Grand children

Singular	Plural	German	Plural
grandchild	grandchildren	das Enkelkind	die Enkelkinder
grandchild	grandchildren	das Kindeskind	die Kindeskinder
granddaughter	granddaughters	die Enkelin	die Enkelinnen
granddaughter	granddaughters	die Enkeltochter	die Enkeltöchter
grandson	grandsons	der Enkel	die Enkel
grandson	grandsons	der Enkelsohn	die Enkelsöhne

Aunts, uncles, cousins, nephews and nieces

singular	plural	German	Plural
aunt	aunties	die Tante	die Tanten
uncle	uncles	der Onkel	die Onkel
cousin (female)	Female cousins	die Cousine	die Cousinen
cousin (male)	male cousins	der Vetter	die Vettern
cousin (female)	Female cousins	die Kusine	die Kusinen
nephew	Nephews	der Neffe	die Neffen
niece	Nieces	die Nichte	die Nichten

In-laws

Singular	Plural	German	Plural
mother-in-law	Mothers-in-law	die Schwiegermutter	die Schwiegermütter
father-in-law	Fathers-in-law	der Schwiegervater	die Schwiegerväter
sister-in-law	Sisters-in-law	die Schwägerin	die Schwägerinnen
brother-in-law	Brothers-in-law	der Schwager	die Schwäger
daughter-in-law	Daughters-in-law	die Schwiegertochter	die Schwiegertöchter
son-in-law	Sons-in-law	der Schwiegersohn	die Schwiegersöhne

Step family

Singular	Plural	German	Plural
stepmother	Stepmothers	die Stiefmutter	die Stiefmütter
stepfather	Stepfathers	der Stiefvater	die Stiefväter
stepdaughter	Stepdaughters	die Stieftochter	die Stieftöchter
stepson	Stepsons	der Stiefsohn	die Stiefsöhne
step brother	Step Brothers	der Stiefbruder	die Stiefbrüder
stepsister	Step Sisters	die Stiefschwester	die Stiefschwestern

12

LEARN OBJECTS IN SPACE AND COMPASS POINTS IN GERMAN

Objects in space

English	German
Stars	die Sterne
Moons	die Monde
Sun	die Sonne
Galaxies	die Galaxien
Nebulas	die Nebel
Comets	die Kometen
Asteroids	die Asteroiden
Meteoroids	die Meteoroiden
Planets	die Planeten
Mercury	der Merkur
Venus	die Venus
Earth	die Erde
Mars	der Mars
Jupiter	der Jupiter
Saturn	der Saturn
Uranus	der Uranus
Neptune	der Neptun
Pluto	der Pluto

Points of the compass

German	English
Norden	north
Nordosten	northeast
Osten	east
Südosten	southeast
Süden	south
Südwesten	southwest
Westen	west
Nordwesten	northwest

Examples in sentences

The sun rises from east to west.
Die Sonne geht von Ost nach West auf.
Jupiter is the largest planet in the solar system.
Jupiter ist der größte Planet des Sonnensystems.
Uranus is the coldest planet.
Uranus ist der käiteste Planet.

13

LEARN COLORS IN GERMAN

	Color	Farbe
	cinnamon	zimt farben
	greenish yellow	grüngelb
	indigo	indigo
	blue	blau
	marine blue, dark blue	Dunkelblau
	yellow	gelb
	cream	cremefarben
	greenish blue	blaugrün
	beige	beige
	sky blue	himmelblau
	khaki	kaki
	white	Weiß
	cyan	grünblau
	maroon	granatrot

	Color	Farbe
	grey	grau
	purple	Violet lila
	orange	orange
	black	schwarz
	jet black	schwarz wie Ebenholz
	red	rot
	Light red	hellrot
	brown	braun
	mahogany	mahagonibraun
	pink	rosa
	dark red	dunkelrot
	violet	violett, veilchen
	green	grün

14

LEARN CONVERSATION STARTERS IN GERMAN

German	English Translation
Danke!	Thank you!
Danke schön!	Thank you very much!
Bitte	Please
Vielen Dank!	Many thanks!
Entschuldigen Sie	Excuse me
Es tut mir leid	I am sorry
Willkommen	Welcome
Grüß Gott!	Hello
Moin!	Hi
Guten Morgen	Good morning
Guten Tag	Good afternoon / good day
Guten Abend	Good evening
Gute Nacht	Good night
Auf Wiedersehen	Good-bye
Bis bald!	See you later
Tschüss!	Bye
Ich heiße..	My name is ….
Mein Name ist..	My name is ….

German	English Translation
Ich bin...	I am.....
Ich komme aus...	I am from...
Heute ist mein erster Tag in....	Today is my first day in ...
Freut mich	Nice to meet you!
Wie geht es Ihnen?	How are you? (formal)
Wie geht es dir?	How are you? (Informal)
Wie geht's?	How are you doing?
Was?	What?
Wo?	Where?
Wann?	When?
Warum?	Why?
Wer?	Who?
Wie?	How?
Wie viel?	How much?
Wie viele?	How many?
Haben Sie ...?	Do you have ...?
Können Sie mir helfen?	Can you help me?
Sprechen Sie Englisch?	Do you speak English?

German	English Translation
Wo finde ich…?	Where do I find…?
Wo ist..?	Where is …?
Wie heißt … auf Deutsch?	How do you say … in German?
Was ist das?	What is this?
Wo sind die Toiletten?	Where are the bathrooms?
Ja	Yes
Nein	No
Ich weiß nicht	I don't know
Ich verstehe nicht	I don't understand
Ich verstehe	I understand
Ich will	I want
Ich will nicht	I don't want
ich suche diese Adresse	I am looking for this address
Es ist auf der anderen Straßenseite	Can you draw it for me?
Wie komme ich dorthin?	How do I get there?
Wo ist die Universität?	Where is the University?
Wie komme ich zum Bahnhof?	How do I get to the train station?
Ist es weit von hier?	Is it far from here
Tschüss, bis zum nächsten Mal	Goodbye, see you next time

AUTHOR'S NOTE: 3

Hey Language Learner, it's Pro Language Learning,

Firstly, thanks for completing our book. This should help put you on the right path.

Remember, there are particular tools that you need not just to help you learn a new language, but to also make it a lot easier.

The first crucial tool you will need to make sure you have so you do not fail is a copy of Master Any Language by Audio Elevate.

When learning any language, the time it takes to go from complete beginner to the level of a native speaker can sometimes take a whole lifetime.

Quite painful to hear, right?

It would be, but luckily for you, I have partnered up with Audio Elevate who are giving away their award-winning book called Master Any Language that will give you all of the step-by-step strategies and fundamentals to learn any language in just a month!

Best thing about this exclusive offer is it is 100 percent FREE, no-strings-attached.

All you need to do to claim your FREE copy of Master Any Language is either click below or type in on your search browsers URL: free.audioelevate.com

Good luck on your journey and enjoy